FAMOUS FIGURES OF

GEORGE CUSTER

THE AMERICAN FRONTIER

FAMOUS FIGURES OF
THE AMERICAN FRONTIER

BILLY THE KID

BUFFALO BILL CODY

CRAZY HORSE

DAVY CROCKETT

GEORGE CUSTER

WYATT EARP

GERONIMO

JESSE JAMES

ANNIE OAKLEY

SITTING BULL

FAMOUS FIGURES OF

GEORGE CUSTER

THE AMERICAN FRONTIER

HAL MARCOVITZ

CHELSEA HOUSE PUBLISHERS
PHILADELPHIA

Produced for Chelsea House by
OTTN Publishing, Stockton, NJ

CHELSEA HOUSE PUBLISHERS
Editor in Chief: Sally Cheney
Associate Editor in Chief: Kim Shinners
Production Manager: Pamela Loos
Art Director: Sara Davis
Series Designer: Keith Trego

First Printing

1 3 5 7 9 8 6 4 2

The Chelsea House World Wide Web address is
http://www.chelseahouse.com

Library of Congress Cataloging-in-Publication Data

Marcovitz, Hal.
George A. Custer / Hal Marcovitz.
p.   cm. – (Famous figures of the American frontier)
Includes bibliographical references and index.
Summary: The life of the Civil War general whose
controversial fame rests chiefly on the disaster at the Little
Big Horn in 1876.
   ISBN 0-7910-6495-6 (alk. paper)
   ISBN 0-7910-6496-4 (pbk.: alk. paper)
1. Custer, George Armstrong, 1839-1876–Juvenile literature.
2. Generals–United States–Biography–Juvenile literature.
3. United States Army–Biography–Juvenile literature.
4. Cheyenne Indians–Wars–Juvenile literature. 5. Little
Bighorn, Battle of the, Mont., 1876–Juvenile literature.
[1. Custer, George Armstrong, 1839-1876. 2. Generals.]
I. Title. II. Series.

E467.1.C99 M37 2001
973.8'2'092–dc21
[B]   2001028848

CONTENTS

Song of the Seventh Cavalry

George A. Custer leads the Seventh Cavalry on a saber-swinging charge against a group of Native Americans. Custer was a dashing cavalry leader who became popular because of his exploits during the Civil War, as well as his adventures after the war fighting Indians in the West.

The soldiers of the Seventh *Cavalry* first heard the song "Garry Owen" as they rode into battle against Cheyenne Indians at the Washita River in Oklahoma on November 27, 1868. The song is a quick march with a lively melody. When Colonel George Armstrong Custer first heard the song, he knew it would stir the emotions of the cavalry soldiers under his command, helping them find the courage to ride into battle.

"We listened intently for the signal notes of 'Garry Owen,' our charging call," wrote Captain Francis M. Gibson, who rode with the Seventh Cavalry at Washita. "At last the inspiring strains of the rollicking tune broke forth, filling the early morning air with joyous music. The profound silence that had reigned through the night was suddenly changed to a pandemonium of tumult and excitement; the wild notes of 'Garry Owen' which had resounded from hill to hill, were answered by wilder shouts of exultation from the charging columns."

The Seventh Cavalry swept into the Cheyenne village as a blinding snowstorm covered the Oklahoma prairie. **Braves** rushed out of their tepees. The Indians attempted to fire back with their rifles and bows and arrows, but they had little success. Custer had caught them sleeping, and now they would pay with their lives. Black Kettle, the Cheyenne chief, was among the 103 Indians killed that morning.

When the battle was over, Custer ordered the tribe's 75 tepees burned to the ground and all the Cheyenne's horses slaughtered. At the start of a bitterly cold Oklahoma winter, Custer had left the survivors no place to live and no horses they could ride to shelter. Later, Custer said he knew women and children would likely be killed in the attack.

"This was quite a delicate mission," Custer wrote, "as it was difficult to convince the squaws and children that they had anything but death to expect at our hands."

The attack was an overwhelming success for Custer's Seventh

The title of Custer's favorite song does not refer to a person named Garry Owen. Instead, the title comes from the Gaelic word *Garryowen*, which means "Owen's Garden." Garryowen is the name of a town near the city of Limerick in Ireland. Many of the soldiers in the U.S. Army were Irish immigrants, who brought their customs and music to their new home in America.

Cavalry—dozens of Indians were killed, while only a handful of cavalry troopers died in the battle. In the years that followed, the U.S. Army would use similar tactics in its war against the Native Americans. Soldiers would ride into Indian villages and wreak *havoc*. They spread gunfire as the surprised and frightened Indians ran for cover. During the mayhem, the troops would fire into tepees and kill women and children as well as braves.

In the upper ranks of the army, such brutal tactics were readily accepted. The men who fought in the Great Plains were praised for their bravery as they decimated the Native American population.

"The energy and rapidity shown during one of the heaviest snowstorms that has visited this section of the country, with the temperatures below the freezing point, and the gallantry and bravery displayed, resulting in such signal success, reflect the highest credit upon both the officers and men of the Seventh Cavalry," wrote Major General Philip H. Sheridan of the battle of Washita.

GARRY OWEN

We are the pride of the army,
   And a regiment of great renown,
Our name's on the pages of history,
   From '66 on down.
If you think we stop or falter,
   While into the fray we're goin'
Just watch the step with our heads erect
   When our band plays Garry Owen.

With their success, the men of the Seventh Cavalry had made their mark as the army's bravest horse soldiers. The Seventh would continue to wage their country's war against the Indians. Each time they rode into battle they would be accompanied by the lively music of "Garry Owen," their commander's favorite song.

Eight years later, this tradition had not changed. At noon on June 22, 1876, the bugles sounded at Fort Abraham Lincoln in North Dakota. Troopers in the Seventh Cavalry mounted their horses, and the *stockade* gates swung open. As the cavalry band played "Garry Owen," the column of 650 cavalry troops behind Custer left the fort and headed west toward Montana and the Little Bighorn River. They had received orders to pursue Indians in that area. The troops were full of confidence, inspired by the words of their commander's favorite song.

Unfortunately, this confidence would not help the Seventh Cavalry three days later. Unknown to Custer and the U.S. Army, the force of Native Americans gathered between the Tongue and Little Bighorn Rivers in Montana was bigger than any *encampment* they had ever seen. Nearly 25,000 Indians were waiting for them, eager for battle.

CUSTER'S LUCK

This view of West Point overlooking the Hudson River was painted in 1861, the year George A. Custer graduated from the military academy there.

any of America's greatest generals have learned the craft of war at the U.S. Military Academy in West Point, New York, which is located along the Hudson River about 50 miles north of New York City.

George Armstrong Custer arrived at West Point in 1857. Certainly, the people who came to know Custer at West Point hardly expected him to become one of the

Future leaders of the United States Army have been trained at West Point since 1802. General Robert E. Lee graduated second in his class from West Point in 1829. He then went on to lead the Confederate army during the Civil War after turning down command of the Union army. That job eventually went to General Ulysses S. Grant, another West Point graduate. Grant would later become the 18th president of the United States.

General John J. Pershing, who led American forces in World War I, graduated from West Point in 1886. General Dwight D. Eisenhower, supreme commander of the Allied forces in World War II, won his diploma from West Point in 1915. Eisenhower also served as president.

military's great leaders. Even Custer had doubts about himself. "My career as a *cadet* had but little to recommend it to the study of those who came after me, unless as an example to be carefully avoided," he wrote years later.

In fact, on June 24, 1861, when Custer was handed his diploma, he had earned the distinction of finishing at the bottom of his class.

༄༅༄༅༄

Custer was born December 5, 1839, in his family's farmhouse in New Rumley, Ohio, a town west of what is now the West Virginia border. There was little in his childhood to suggest a destiny as a great cavalry leader. He did, however, find himself sitting atop a horse at a very early age. His father, Emanuel Henry Custer, was a farmer and blacksmith. He often placed young George on the back of freshly *shod* horses. Custer's mother, Mary Ward Custer, was a typical 19th-century farmer's wife. She worked hard to keep the household running and to take care of the family.

Custer's birth marked the beginning of what everyone who knew him would call "Custer's luck" —his uncanny ability to take advantage of a turn of good fortune. Before George was born, Emanuel and Mary had lost two infant children in childbirth. This was a common occurrence in the days before the great advances in medicine of the 20th century. George was the first of the Custer children to survive childbirth. Later, he was followed by a sister and two brothers. In fact, his brother Tom would go on to a valiant military career as well, winning the Congressional Medal of Honor in the Civil War.

George's father enjoyed sharing a good practical joke with his sons. "I was always a boy with the boys," Emanuel Custer once said. One time, on a train trip, the boys locked Emanuel out of his compartment. As he pounded on the door and

Everyone in the Custer family called young George Custer "Autie." The little blond-haired boy had made that sound while trying to pronounce his middle name, Armstrong.

demanded to be let back in, the boys surprised their father by dumping a bucket of ice water on his head. Later, Emanuel struck back by accusing the boys of picking his pocket. An angry crowd descended on the frightened Custer boys until Emanuel, laughing, confessed that it was all a joke.

And so a fun-loving, carefree son of Emanuel Custer found himself at the gates of West Point in 1857, hardly ready for the stern discipline and rigors of cavalry training that awaited him.

By the time he graduated, Custer had earned 700 *demerits*. He was nearly kicked out because of his wild behavior. He showed up for class unshaven or with his red-yellow hair uncombed. His uniform was often dirty and wrinkled. He rarely shined his boots. He never learned how to salute properly. He was regularly punished by being forced to march guard duty on West Point's parade grounds. "I devoted sixty-six Saturday afternoons to this method of vindicating outraged military law during my cadetship of four years," Custer wrote.

Still, Custer insisted on having his fun. He found ways to sneak out of the **barracks** after **taps** for a night on the town. He gambled with other cadets. He was habitually late for class. And he was hardly a dedicated student. Custer never seemed to have the time or patience for studying.

However, he was good at practical jokes. One time, during Spanish class, he asked the teacher to translate "class dismissed" into Spanish. When the teacher obliged, Cadet Custer led his classmates out the door. Another time, he told a professor that he hadn't done his homework because he was busy the night before. He was swimming across the Hudson River to win a bet. In the wintertime, he kept snow-balls in his saddlebag and tossed them at people.

George Custer's younger brother, Thomas Ward Custer, also attended West Point. Like his older brother, Tom Custer would go on to a distinguished military career. He won the Congressional Medal of Honor during the Civil War.

"He was a reckless cadet, always in trouble, always playing some mischievous pranks, and liked by everyone," wrote one of his classmates, J. M. Wright. When Wright first met him, Custer was walking onto the West Point campus after returning from leave. Nearly everyone was remarking, "Here comes Custer!"

Cadet Tully McCrea, Custer's roommate at West Point, wrote that Custer "was always connected with mischief that was going on. He never studies any more than he can possibly help." But McCrea also wrote that he admired Custer and "envied his free and careless way, and the perfect indifference he had for everything. It was all right whether he knew his lesson or not; he did not allow it to trouble him."

But Custer had a good heart. He was one of the best fighters on the West Point campus, and he once gave a bully a black eye for picking on a smaller cadet. And he was very serious about the lessons he took in horsemanship. "I take lessons in riding every day, and this I enjoy very much," Custer wrote to a friend. By the time he left West Point, Custer was regarded as the best horseman in his class.

He was at or near the bottom of the class in almost everything else, though. He finished fifth

This portrait photograph of George Custer was taken while he was a cadet at West Point. Custer was not an outstanding student, graduating at the bottom of his class in 1861. However, he took his courses in horsemanship and in fighting very seriously. These would help him during his military career.

from the bottom in cavalry tactics, third from the bottom in strategy, and last in general studies. He barely passed his final exams. Of the 34 cadets who received diplomas at West Point in June 1861, Custer was 34th in class rank. "Well, somebody had to be last, and I earned the dubious distinction," Custer wrote later.

But at the time, class rank wasn't so important to the U.S. Army. In April, conflict had broken out between the states of the North and the South—the Civil War. Young officers were needed on the front lines, and it didn't much matter whether they finished at the top of the class or the bottom.

This portrait of Custer hangs in the U.S. Military Academy at West Point. Although Custer's graduation rank was low, he proved himself a more than capable leader during the Civil War, becoming at age 23 the youngest general in the Union army.

THE BOY GENERAL

Lieutenant George Custer reported for duty on July 21, 1861, with the Second Cavalry outside Centerville, Virginia. The unit was preparing for the battle of Bull Run, the first major conflict of the Civil War. In fact, the battle started just hours after Custer arrived in camp.

The battle of Bull Run (sometimes called the battle of Manassas) proved to be a disaster for the Union army. It showed just how unprepared and poorly trained the Union soldiers were for battle.

The Civil War had been brewing for a long time. In late 1860, after the election of Abraham Lincoln as president of the United States, the legislature of South Carolina voted to *secede*, or withdraw, from the Union. Other Southern states followed, claiming that the U.S. government no longer represented their interests. In April 1861, Southern forces attacked Fort Sumter in South Carolina. President Lincoln called for a large army to put down the *rebellion*. At Bull Run, the first major battle of the Civil War, most of the Union soldiers were untrained recruits.

Custer rode with the Second Cavalry's Company G, which had been ordered to support *infantry* troops attempting to take a hill. But before Company G's charge up the hill even started, a flood of Union troops poured out of a nearby woods in retreat. Custer's men had no choice but to join the retreat.

It was a rude and bitter introduction to battle for the young lieutenant, who had left West Point with gallant visions of himself leading cavalry charges against rebel forces. Instead, he was forced to participate in a humiliating defeat, never even getting a chance to fire a shot at the enemy.

Later, Custer wrote: "One who has never witnessed the conduct of large numbers of men, when seized by a panic such as that was, cannot realize how utterly senseless and without apparent reason men will act. And yet the same men may have exhibited great gallantry and intelligence but a moment before."

President Abraham Lincoln demanded a change after Bull Run. He placed General George B. McClellan in charge of the Union army, ordering him to properly train the men and prepare them for a long war against the soldiers of the South, called the Confederates. McClellan, known to his men as "Little Mac," waited eight months before moving his force of 100,000 men south to march on Richmond, Virginia, the capital of the Confederate States of America.

Custer was thrilled by the appointment of McClellan, a general he admired. "I have more confidence in General McClellan than in any man living," Custer wrote. "I would forsake everything and follow him to the ends of the Earth. I would lay down my life for him. Every officer and private worships him. The greatest expedition ever fitted is going south under the greatest and best of men. We

After the disastrous and embarrassing defeat of the Union army at Bull Run, President Abraham Lincoln appointed General George B. McClellan to take command of the army. McClellan turned out to be a great organizer, building and training a large force of 100,000 soldiers. However, he was criticized for moving too slowly against the rebels.

are not certain whither we are bound, but are confident this will be Richmond."

The advance began in May 1862. McClellan moved his men south from Washington to the *peninsula* between the James and York Rivers below Richmond. He then began an advance north toward the capital. During the march north, Custer distinguished himself in battle, leading cavalry charges against the rebels. His commander, General Winfield Scott Hancock, often wrote: "Lieutenant Custer, Fifth Regular Cavalry, volunteered and led the way on horseback." Such reports came to the attention of General McClellan.

McClellan's army had to fight its way north against a rebel force under the leadership of General Joseph E. Johnston. On May 22, 1862, Custer was a member of a scouting party riding ahead of McClellan's army, seeking a path through the swampy Virginia countryside. Suddenly, the scouts arrived at the boggy banks of the Chickahominy River. To continue the pursuit against Johnston's army, the Union soldiers would have to find a way to cross the Chickahominy. Other officers in the scouting party suggested searching downriver for a way to cross.

Custer knew that would delay the advance, allowing Johnston's army time to escape. So the young lieutenant jumped off his horse, drew his pistol, and waded into the swampy river. It was a brash and perhaps foolish move. By wading into the river, Custer had exposed himself to *sniper* fire. But Custer's luck held again. He was able to wade across the river and back, proving that the Chickahominy was shallow enough to cross and there was no need to find an alternate route downriver.

When Custer and the scouting party returned to camp, he was summoned to McClellan's headquarters. The general was clearly impressed by the bold move of this young officer, just a few months out of West Point.

"Custer was simply a reckless, gallant boy undeterred by fatigue, unconscious of fear; but his head was always clear in danger . . . I became much attached to him," McClellan wrote.

McClellan promoted Custer to captain and transferred him to his staff, appointing him *aide-de-camp*. Custer would now serve as an assistant to the general. He would help advise Little Mac on strategy and tactics, carry out McClellan's commands, and serve as the general's personal scout.

Custer worked hard for McClellan. He led successful assaults on Southern cavalry troops at the battles of White Oak Swamp, Seven Pines, and Antietam. But by late fall in 1862, McClellan still hadn't marched on Richmond. And so on November 5, Lincoln relieved McClellan of command of the Union army. When McClellan was fired, it meant the officers on his staff were dismissed from their jobs as well. Custer returned to Monroe, Michigan, where he had made his home before his West Point years, to await further orders.

He arrived in Monroe weary, deeply depressed, and unsure of his future in the army.

During a visit home while he was waiting to be given new orders, George Custer met Elizabeth "Libby" Clift Bacon. The two fell in love and were married before the end of the war.

But his spirits were soon raised. Shortly after arriving in Monroe, Custer met Elizabeth Clift Bacon. He called her "Libby," and they would be married before the end of the war.

"He is a simple, frank manly fellow," Libby's cousin Rebecca wrote of Custer. "And he fairly idolizes Libby. I am sure he will make her a true, noble husband. . . . They cannot but be happy."

Meanwhile, Custer had to wait until April 1863 before returning to duty. The Union army was now under the command of General Joseph Hooker, known as "Fighting Joe Hooker" in the newspapers of the era. Custer was assigned to the staff of General Alfred Pleasonton, one of Hooker's cavalry commanders.

It would not be a triumphant return to battle for Custer. Soon after Custer joined Pleasonton's staff, the Union army suffered terrible losses at the battle of the Rappahannock River. But two months later, Custer led a successful cavalry charge against a *crack* mounted force under the command of a famed Confederate general, J. E. B. Stuart.

Stuart's cavalry troops had continually harassed Union forces throughout the war. In fact, the Union soldiers had grudgingly nicknamed Stuart's men the "Invincibles." But on June 9, 1863, Custer's men surprised a force of Stuart's Invincibles near Brandy Station, Virginia, and cut them down. It would not be the last time in the war that George Custer would go head to head against Stuart. The successful charge against the Invincibles prompted General Hooker to praise Custer for his "gallantry through-out the fight."

But despite Custer's valor, as well as the heroics of many other Union soldiers and officers, the Union army was still unable to break through the rebel defenses and march on Richmond. Lincoln blamed his generals. Not until the president installed General Ulysses S. Grant at the head of the army later in 1863 would the Union forces find success in what became known as the Peninsular Campaign.

In the meantime, the president was continually forced to shuffle the army's commanders, hoping that someone would come up with a way to break through. As a result, many young officers found themselves quickly moving up in rank. One of those officers was George Armstrong Custer.

On June 27, 1863, in yet another shake-up ordered by Lincoln, General George Meade replaced Fighting Joe Hooker as head of the Union army. Meade resolved to appoint young, fiery officers to important posts, hoping their dash and heroism would spark the army to victory. When Meade approached Pleasonton and asked him to recommend such an officer, Pleasonton immediately suggested Custer.

On June 29, 1863, Captain Custer was suddenly promoted to the rank of brigadier general. Certainly, the bold move by Custer's superiors shocked Custer as well as his former classmates at West Point. They undoubtedly remembered how Custer never took his studies seriously, constantly marched guard duty as punishment, and finished at the bottom of the class. Custer was 23 years old, the

Custer was promoted to brigadier general just days before the battle of Gettysburg. He won his greatest glory during the pivotal conflict, leading his Union cavalry on two successful skirmishes against the Confederate cavalry of J. E. B. Stuart.

youngest man promoted to the rank of general in the history of the United States Army.

He soon became known as the "Boy General." Upon learning of his promotion, Custer raced off to have himself fitted for a new uniform, fashioned out of blue and black velvet fabric. Custer had also started wearing his blond hair quite long–longer than the commanders of the U.S. Army were used to seeing on their officers. The long hair and fancy uniform served to add to his reputation as a brash and *flamboyant* officer. "I wanted to wear a distinctive uniform so that my men would know where I was on the battle line," Custer wrote later.

Custer led cavalry troops throughout the remainder of the Civil War and scored impressive victories. During the final six months of the war, Custer's cavalry soldiers captured 111 cannons and other pieces of artillery equipment, 65 battle flags, and 10,000 Confederate prisoners.

He found his greatest glory at the command of the First Michigan Cavalry, leading his men at the pivotal battle of Gettysburg in Pennsylvania. In this bloody three-day battle, the tide of the war was finally turned in favor of the Union army. During the battle, Custer led two attacks against J. E. B. Stuart's Invincibles, winning both *skirmishes*.

He wrote: "I cannot find language to express my high appreciation of the gallantry and daring displayed by the officers and men of the First Michigan Cavalry. They advanced to the charge of a vastly superior force with as much order and precision as if going on parade, and I challenge the annals of warfare to produce a more brilliant or successful charge of cavalry."

A column of cavalry, artillery, and wagons crossing the plains of the Dakota Territory in 1874. This group of soldiers, commanded by Custer, was making an expedition into South Dakota's Black Hills, in violation of a peace treaty that had been signed with the Sioux six years earlier.

LONG HAIR

The Civil War ended in 1865, but Custer still regarded himself as a fighting man. And in America's untamed western territories, there would be no shortage of work for fighting men in the years to come.

Before the war, there had been trouble in the western territories. Native Americans had been attacking settlers and gold miners. During the war, the government could do little about the attacks, since most of its troops had been sent south to fight the rebels. Now that the war was over, the government turned its attention fully on what officials in Washington called the Indian problem.

Custer's assignment following the war was to head a new mounted fighting unit of the U.S. Army—the Seventh Cavalry. Shortly after the war, Custer had been reduced in rank to lieutenant colonel. It was not uncommon for officers who had been promoted during wartime to be demoted once peace had been declared. He was still young for this rank—when he took over the Seventh Cavalry, Custer was 27 years old.

The Seventh would be based at Fort Riley in Kansas, about 100 miles west of Kansas City. George and Libby Custer arrived at Fort Riley in October 1866. By the following March, the Seventh was assigned to tame hostile Cheyenne Indians in Kansas. Custer did not expect the Indians to put up much of a fight. While on the trail, he wrote to Libby: "I do not anticipate war, or even difficulty, as the Indians are frightened to death."

But the assignment was not as easy as Custer expected. During the Civil War, Custer was accus-

Here is how Custer once described a surprise Indian attack on the Seventh Cavalry's camp:

> It was just that uncertain period between darkness and daylight on the following morning, and I was lying in my tent deep in the enjoyment of that perfect repose which only camp life offers when the sharp, clear crack of a carbine nearby brought me to my feet. I knew in an instant that the shot came from the picket posted not far from the rear of my camp. At the same moment my brother, who on that occasion was officer of the day, and whose duties required him to be particularly on the alert, rushed past my tent, halting only long enough to show his face through the opening and shout, "They are here!"
>
> Now I did not inquire who were referred to, or how many were included in the word "they," nor did my informant seem to think it necessary to explain. "They" referred to Indians, I knew full well. Had I doubted, the brisk fusillade which opened the next moment, and the wild war-whoop, were convincing evidences that in truth "They were here!"

tomed to leading charges against opposing rebel cavalries. The two sides would usually smash into each other at full gallop. The fight would often be won by the force with superior numbers, with the most clever tactics, or with the best leadership. That is not how wars were fought against the Indians on the Great Plains. The Indians would strike quickly, then disappear into the fog of night or the wilderness. They knew the territories much better than their pursuers, and they proved to be quite difficult to track down.

The Native Americans weren't Custer's only problem on the Plains. In 1867 Custer was *court-martialed* for leaving his duties to visit his wife. He was sentenced to a one-year suspension without pay. However, by the fall of 1868 he had been reinstated as commander of the Seventh Cavalry. The Plains Indians were increasingly hostile, and Custer was needed.

The Seventh Cavalry would strike back like lightning, winning their first great battle against the Indians at the battle of Washita. On August 17, 1868, a group of Cheyenne Indians had attacked a white settlement in Kansas. The Seventh Cavalry was ordered to retaliate. For months, the Seventh pursued the Cheyenne, finally catching up with them the night of November 26 on the banks of the Washita River in Oklahoma Territory, west of Kansas. It was a bitterly cold night. Snow had come early to Oklahoma, and Custer found the Cheyenne huddled in their tepees.

The cavalry spent hours getting into position, surrounding the village. Custer ordered the Seventh Cavalry's band to play "Garry Owen." And then, in the early morning hours of November 27, he ordered the attack. The inspired cavalry surprised the Cheyenne, finding them asleep in their tepees and unprepared for the battle.

Custer's lopsided victory at the battle of Washita earned him the respect and praise of his superiors. It also earned him *infamy* among the Indians. Following the battle, Indians across the western territories told the story of the brutal attack of the Seventh Cavalry. They described how the horse soldiers were led by a young and flamboyant

The Seventh Cavalry charges into Black Kettle's village on the Washita River in November 1868.

commander who wore his red-yellow hair to his shoulders. They called Custer "Long Hair."

Certainly, the Indians unlucky enough to find themselves in the way of the Seventh Cavalry were often made to pay with their lives. And members of the Seventh Cavalry soon learned that their commander was not a man to cross, as his punishments could be harsh and unforgiving.

As a cadet at West Point, and as a battlefield commander in the Civil War, Custer had a reputation as a risk-taking, fun-loving young officer not opposed to breaking the rules when it suited him. But his attitude changed while commanding the Seventh Cavalry. He became a stern *disciplinarian*, ordering rule-breakers whipped or imprisoned in uncomfortable jail cells dug as pits in the earth. He refused to tolerate drunkenness in the ranks. The sentries at Fort Riley were ordered to shoot *deserters*.

Custer believed the harsh rules were needed to combat desertion, which was a major problem for army commanders on the Plains. Custer feared many of his men would leave the army without permission to seek fortunes as gold miners.

"The opportunity to obtain marvelous wages as

miners and the prospect of amassing sudden wealth proved a temptation sufficiently strong to make many of the men forget their sworn obligations to their government and their duties as soldiers," he wrote. "Forgetting for the moment that the command to which they belonged was actually engaged in war and was in a country infested with armed bodies of the enemy, and that the legal penalty of desertion under such circumstances was death, many of the men formed a combination to desert their colors and escape to the mines."

On the Plains, the Seventh Cavalry was soon assigned the duty of protecting surveyors who were trying to lay a course for the railroad across Indian lands. One of those railroads was planned to cross an area of South Dakota known as the Black Hills.

A Good Day to Die

This painting, *Call of the Bugle*, depicts Custer's Last Stand—the general and his men trying to hold off an overwhelming force of hostile Native Americans. While the Last Stand may have been brave, Custer's decision to split his force and attack was foolish. He ignored reports by his scouts that the Indian camp on the Little Bighorn was much larger than expected.

The most vicious and bloody war waged between the Indians of the Plains and the U.S. Army was the War for the Black Hills.

The roots of the war could be found in the Indian Removal Act, a law signed in 1830 by President Andrew Jackson. The law gave the United States government the authority to forcibly remove Indians from their lands.

Thousands of Indians were forced off their forested and fertile lands and made to live in strange territories, or on barren *reservations* the government had set aside for them. Often, buffalo were scarce on the reservations, forcing the Indians to rely on meager rations the government promised but often failed to deliver.

Jackson was responding to his nation's desire for "Manifest Destiny," the belief that the United States should push its borders all the way to the shores of the Pacific Ocean on the west coast. Usually, that meant pushing Indians out of the way and taking their land for settlement by white men.

Some Indians resigned themselves to the fate that awaited them on the reservations. But many did not go willingly and chose to make war.

When settlers, gold miners, and railroad men arrived in the Black Hills of South Dakota, the Hunkpapa Sioux under their great chief, Sitting Bull, vowed to drive them away. The Sioux called the Black Hills "Paha Sapa." They believed the region in western South Dakota to be the most sacred of their lands, the center of their world. In the Sioux language, the words *Paha Sapa* mean "Hills that are black." The hills form a dark, mountainous mass that rises some 4,000 feet into the sky, providing a stark contrast to the yellow prairies that surround them. The Black Hills had great spiritual significance for the Sioux. Paha Sapa was a holy place where warriors could speak with Wakan Tanka, the Great Spirit.

"We want no white men here," Sitting Bull said. "The Black Hills belong to me. If the whites try to take them, I will fight."

In Washington, the nation's leaders were becoming impatient

Sitting Bull was a respected war leader and medicine man of the Hunkpapa Sioux. He organized his people to defend the Black Hills, which the Sioux considered sacred ground, from whites who wanted to mine the land for gold.

with the Native Americans. They wanted railroads built across Indian lands in the Plains. A new route west known as the Bozeman Trail had been opened through Sioux lands in Wyoming and Montana. America's leaders wanted settlers to use the trail without fear of Indian attacks. What's more, gold had been discovered in the Black Hills. When Sitting Bull was asked by the federal government to permit gold mining in the Black Hills, he flatly refused.

On January 31, 1876, Edward P. Smith, the commissioner of Indian Affairs, ordered the Sioux to move to a reservation in North and South Dakota. They had to abandon the Black Hills or face military action. Again, the Sioux refused.

On March 17, the first shots were fired in the War for the Black Hills. A column led by Colonel Joseph J. Reynolds attacked a village of Oglala Sioux near the Powder River in Montana. The Oglalas feared more attacks, so their chief, Crazy Horse, moved his tribe west to the Tongue River, where Sitting Bull and the Hunkpapas were camped. They were joined by a tribe of Cheyenne Indians.

Custer very nearly missed the War for the Black Hills. In March 1876, he testified before Congress about *corruption* and fraud in the War Department's handling of Indian affairs. President Grant was furious with Custer and relieved him of command.

Only a popular outcry made Grant change his mind and allow Custer to rejoin the Seventh Cavalry.

By June 1876, many historians believe, there were 25,000 Indians camped between the Tongue and Little Bighorn Rivers in Montana. Whether the army and, in particular, George Custer knew there was such a *formidable* force of Indians at the Little Bighorn remains the subject of a debate that has never been settled.

Nevertheless, the army hatched a plan to once and for all settle the Indian problem. The army decided to send three forces of soldiers into Montana for a showdown with the Sioux and Cheyenne. The forces were led by General George Crook, General Alfred Terry, and Colonel John Gibbon. Custer and the Seventh Cavalry served under Terry.

Crook's army met up with Crazy Horse and the Oglala Sioux on the night of June 17 on the banks of the Rosebud River, just east of the Little Bighorn. Most of the battle was fought in darkness. Men scuffled hand to hand under the confusing veil of the moonless Montana night. By dawn Crook had been defeated. Crazy Horse watched in triumph as Crook's troopers left the battlefield in retreat.

Custer and the Seventh were based at Fort Abraham Lincoln just south of Bismarck, North Dakota. On June 22, General Terry issued orders to Custer, directing the Seventh Cavalry to pursue Indians in the area between the Rosebud and Little Bighorn Rivers.

In his orders, Terry made it clear Custer should decide for himself what action to take if he found hostile Indians. "It is impossible to give you any definite instructions . . . and were it not impossible to do so, the commander places too much confidence in your zeal, energy and ability to wish to impose upon you precise orders which might hamper your action when nearly in contact with the enemy," Terry wrote.

Crow Indian scouts riding with the Seventh Cavalry warned Custer he would be attacking an overwhelming force of Sioux and Cheyenne. Custer chose not to believe them. One of the scouts, Bloody Knife, made a sign as the sun rose on the 25th, and said that he would not see it set.

On the afternoon of June 25, as the Seventh Cavalry approached the Little Bighorn, Custer split the cavalry into three columns. He would lead 264 men on an attack from the east. A second column of about 150 men

The great Oglala Sioux warrior Crazy Horse is pictured near the center of this drawing wearing a single feather in his hair. He is riding hard to chase down soldiers of the Seventh Cavalry. Crazy Horse cut off Custer's attempt to retreat, forcing him into his "Last Stand" on a hill overlooking the river.

under Major Marcus Reno would attack from the south. A third column under Major Frederick Benteen would arrive last, providing aid to the columns under Custer and Reno.

Reno's troops arrived first, flooding into a Hunkpapa village on the banks of the Little Bighorn. They were met by Hunkpapa warriors under a chief named Gall, and Oglala warriors under Crazy Horse. Reno's men were quickly routed. The Indian warriors drove them back across

This diorama, part of the collection at the Little Bighorn Battlefield National Monument, shows Major Marcus Reno and his men retreating from the Sioux village, pursued by Sitting Bull's braves. Reno's soldiers crossed the Little Bighorn and halted at a bluff overlooking the river, where they held off the Native Americans until the next evening.

the river, where they were lucky to escape with just 18 killed and 46 wounded.

"I was lying in my lodge," Sitting Bull said. "Some young men ran in to me and said, 'They are firing into the camp.' I jumped up and stepped out of my lodge. The old men, the women, and the children were hurried away. There was great confusion. The women were like flying birds; the bullets were like humming bees. I said to the men:

'Warriors, we have everything to fight for, and if we are defeated we shall have nothing to live for; therefore, let us fight like brave men.' "

Black Elk, who was a young Hunkpapa boy at the time of the battle, later said, "Out of the dust came soldiers on their big horses. They looked big and strong and tall and they were all shooting. My brother took his gun and yelled for me to go back. Then, another great cry went up out of the dust: Crazy Horse is coming! Crazy Horse is coming!"

Custer's men arrived a short time later, just north of where Reno's troopers had been turned away. This time, there would be no Custer's luck.

Just before the charge of the Seventh Cavalry, Custer ordered the band to play "Garry Owen." The troopers rode east toward the Little Bighorn, planning to cross the shallow river to attack the Hunkpapa village on the other side. They never got that far. Custer's men found themselves caught on a hill overlooking the Little Bighorn River. They were completely surrounded by warriors.

"I never before nor since saw men so brave and fearless as those white warriors," an Oglala chief named Low Dog later recalled. "We retreated until our men all got together and then we charged upon them. I called to my men, 'This is a good day to die. Follow me!' As we rushed upon them, the white warriors dismounted to fire, but they did very poor shooting. They held their horses' reins on one arm while they were shooting, but the horses were so frightened that they pulled men all around, and a great many of their shots went up in the air and did us no harm."

Across the river, Indians watching the battle from the Hunkpapa village later said they lost sight of the soldiers because the dust and gun smoke was so heavy. All 264 men who rode that day under the command of George Armstrong Custer were killed at the battle of the Little Bighorn. When it became clear that they could not fight their way off the hill, some of the troopers threw down their rifles and begged for mercy. But they were shown no mercy that afternoon.

After the battle, many Indians who participated said they didn't know who among them had killed Custer. Sitting Bull later said that Custer was the last man to die.

"I tell no lies about dead men," Sitting Bull said. "These men who came with Long Hair were as good men as ever fought. When they rode up, their

Native Americans leave the battlefield after the battle of the Little Bighorn. Although the defeat of Custer's troops was perhaps the greatest Sioux victory, it led to an increased effort by the U.S. government to force the Indians onto reservations.

horses were tired and they were tired. When they got off from their horses, they could not stand firmly on their feet. They swayed to and fro, like the limbs of cypresses in a great wind. Some of them staggered under the weight of their guns. But they began to fight at once. But by this time, our camps were aroused, and there were plenty of warriors to meet them. Our young men rained lead across the river and drove the white braves back."

"A Sad and Terrible Blunder"

White stones mark the spots where Seventh Cavalry troopers fell during the battle of the Little Bighorn. The site of the battle is now a national park visited by thousands of people each year.

ajor Benteen's men never made it to the Little Bighorn. They encountered Reno's men in retreat, and followed them to safety in some nearby hills.

Reno became the scapegoat of the battle. Army investigators concluded that his men gave up too quickly. Even Sitting Bull agreed. Years later, he said, "Squaws and papooses could have dealt with Reno."

Following the battle, Sitting Bull sent braves into the hills after Reno and Benteen. But after some minor skirmishes with the cavalry soldiers, Sitting Bull ordered the braves to withdraw.

"Let them go," he said. "They have come against us, and we have killed a few. If we kill them all, they will send a bigger army after us."

That is just what the army intended. After the embarrassing defeat at the Little Bighorn, the army flooded Montana, North Dakota, and South Dakota with soldiers. Hundreds of Indians were killed by soldiers who vowed to avenge the slaughter of the Seventh Cavalry.

Soon, the Sioux under Sitting Bull were driven north into Canada. The Indians were able to live in safety there, but the hunting was poor and the winters bitterly cold. After five years Sitting Bull led his weary people back into Montana, where they surrendered their weapons and agreed to live on a reservation. The War for the Black Hills was over. Never again would the Plains Indians defeat the U.S. Army in battle.

Custer's body was recovered from the battlefield and buried at West Point. He was 36 years old at the time of his death.

Captain Benteen

It was well known that Captain Frederick W. Benteen disliked Custer, his superior officer. Some historians have speculated that Benteen purposely did not ride to Custer's aid, instead joining Reno's men in the hills above the Little Bighorn. Major Marcus A. Reno had been a capable officer during the Civil War. However, he lacked Indian-fighting experience. His disorganized retreat made him a scapegoat for Custer's defeat.

Major Reno

Libby Custer learned of her husband's death on July 6, 1876, when the wounded men from Major Reno's column arrived back at Fort Abraham Lincoln. She was one of 26 army wives at Fort Lincoln who lost their husbands at the battle of the Little Bighorn.

The widow of Colonel Custer later wrote about that day. She said, "At that very hour, the fears that our tortured minds had portrayed in imagination were realities. The sun rose on a beautiful world, but with its earliest beams came the first knell of disaster. The battle wrecked the lives of twenty-six women at Fort Lincoln, and orphaned children and officers and soldiers joined the cry to that of their bereaved mothers. From that time the life went out of the hearts of the women who weep, and God asked them to walk on alone and in shadow."

> Libby Custer outlived her husband by 56 years. She died in 1933 at the age of 90. She never married again, and she defended her husband and his decision to attack at the Little Bighorn until the day of her death. She is buried at West Point, next to the grave of her husband.

The army spent years investigating the foolish charge of the Seventh Cavalry but found no easy answers.

General Alfred Terry, whose orders left it up to Custer to decide the best course of action at the Little Bighorn, claimed that Custer never should have attacked.

"It was a sad and terrible blunder," Terry wrote of the attack. "For whatever errors he may have committed, he had paid the penalty."

Major General Philip H. Sheridan, who had praised Custer for his victory at the Washita River, believed that Custer had underestimated the force of Indians camped at the Little Bighorn. "I do not attribute Colonel Custer's action to either reckless-ness or want of judgment, but to a misapprehension of the situation and to a superabundance of courage," he said.

Still, others believed Custer was a glory-seeker. They thought he hoped to be the cavalry officer who took the initiative and solved the nation's Indian problem. "He preferred to make a reckless dash and take the consequences rather than share the glory with others," read an editorial in the *Chicago Tribune.* "He took the risk, and he lost."

Ulysses S. Grant, the great Civil War general who had become president of the United States, said, "I regard Custer's massacre as a sacrifice of troops, brought on by Custer himself, that was wholly unnecessary–wholly unnecessary."

Whether or not Custer was entirely to blame for the Seventh Cavalry's devastating defeat at the Little Bighorn has never been determined. Although his decision to attack at the Little Bighorn cost him and his men their lives, it gained Custer immortality. The dashing, reckless officer who finished at the bottom of his class at West Point remains one of America's most well-known military figures.

CHRONOLOGY

1830 President Andrew Jackson signs the Indian Removal Act, giving power to the United States government to forcibly move Indians from their lands

1839 George Armstrong Custer is born in New Rumley, Ohio, on December 5

1857 Enrolls at the U.S. Military Academy in West Point, New York

1861 Graduates from West Point at the bottom of his class on June 24; reports for duty with the Second Cavalry on July 21 and immediately fights in the battle of Bull Run, a defeat for the Union army

1862 Promoted to captain in May and named an aide-de-camp to General George B. McClellan, commander of the Union army; on November 5, President Lincoln relieves McClellan of command; Custer returns home to Monroe, Michigan, to await new orders

1863 In April, Custer is assigned to the staff of General Alfred Pleasonton; on June 9, Custer's cavalry soldiers defeat a Confederate cavalry force under J. E. B. Stuart at Brandy Station, Virginia; on June 29, Custer is promoted to brigadier general, becoming the youngest general in the history of the United States

1864 Marries Elizabeth "Libby" Clift Bacon on February 9

1865 The Civil War ends

1868 Leads the Seventh Cavalry to its first victory over the Plains Indians at the battle of Washita in Oklahoma on November 17

1876 On January 31, Edward P. Smith, commissioner of Indian Affairs, orders Sioux Indians to move onto a reservation in North and South Dakota or face military action; the Sioux refuse; on March 17, the U.S. Army attacks the Oglala Sioux at the battle of the Powder River in Montana; on June 17, soldiers serving under General George Crook are defeated at the battle of the Rosebud River in Montana; Custer and 264 of his men are killed at the battle of the Little Bighorn in Montana on June 25

1881 The land where the battle of the Little Bighorn was fought is designated a national memorial

1991 The name of the park is changed from Custer Battlefield to Little Bighorn Battlefield National Memorial

1999 Ground is broken for an Indian Memorial at the Little Bighorn Battlefield National Memorial

GLOSSARY

aide-de-camp—an officer who acts as an assistant to another officer of higher rank.

barracks—a building used to house soldiers.

brave—a Native American warrior.

cavalry—soldiers mounted on horses.

cadet—a student at a military school.

corruption—improper conduct while in a position of power, such as bribery or the selling of favors.

court-martial—to try a member of the armed forces according to the rules of military justice.

crack—highly trained; of superior ability.

demerits—marks against one's record for breaking the rules.

deserter—a person who leaves his or her military duty without permission and without intending to return.

disciplinarian—a person who enforces the rules closely.

encampment—the place where a group, such as a troop of soldiers, takes temporary residence in a camp.

flamboyant—given to striking, colorful, or outlandish behavior.

formidable—impressive, strong, or difficult to defeat.

havoc—chaos, destruction.

infamy—a bad reputation caused by shocking or criminal behavior; disgrace.

infantry—soldiers who fight on foot.

peninsula—an area of land surrounded by water on three sides, with the fourth side connected to a larger body of land.

rebellion–open, armed defiance of or resistance to an established government.

reservation–a piece of public land set aside where Native Americans were forced live.

secede–to withdraw from an organization, political group, or federation.

shod–fitted with horseshoes.

skirmish–a minor fight during a war.

sniper–someone who shoots at enemy soldiers from a concealed spot.

stockade–an enclosure surrounded by a wall made of wooden posts or stakes.

taps–a military bugle call played at night or at funerals.

FURTHER READING

Bachrach, Deborah. *Custer's Last Stand.* San Diego: Greenhaven Press Inc., 1990.

Brennan, Kristine. *Crazy Horse.* Philadelphia: Chelsea House Publishers, 2002.

Brown, Dee. *Bury My Heart at Wounded Knee.* New York: Bantam Books, 1972.

Connell, Evan S. *Son of the Morning Star: Custer and the Little Bighorn.* San Francisco: North Point Press, 1984.

Gildart, Bert. "Two Sides of Little Bighorn." *Historic Traveler* 1, no. 2 (Summer 2001): 24-29.

Kinsley, D. A. *Custer: Favor the Bold.* New York: Promontory Press, 1992.

Marcovitz, Hal. *Sitting Bull.* Philadelphia: Chelsea House Publishers, 2002.

Shields, Charles J. *Buffalo Bill Cody.* Philadelphia: Chelsea House Publishers, 2002.

Viola, Herman J. *It Is a Good Day to Die.* New York: Crown Publishers Inc., 1998.

PICTURE CREDITS

HAL MARCOVITZ is a journalist for the *Allentown Morning Call* in Pennsylvania. His other titles for Chelsea House include biographies of the explorers Marco Polo and Francisco Coronado, the Indian guide Sacajawea, and the Apollo astronauts. He lives in Chalfont, Pennsylvania, with his wife, Gail, and daughters Ashley and Michelle.